Wireless Netw...

Location:

Wireless Network:

Password:

Location:

Wireless Network:

Password:

Location:

Wireless Network:

Password:

Location:

Wireless Network:

Password:

Location:

Wireless Network:

Password:

Location:

Wireless Network:

Password:

A

Account:

Username:

Password:

Email:

Pin Code:

Security Question:

Answer:

Account:

Username:

Password:

Email:

Pin Code:

Security Question:

Answer:

Account:

Username:

Password:

Email:

Pin Code:

Security Question:

Answer:

A

Account:

Username:

Password:

Email:

Pin Code:

Security Question:

Answer:

Account:

Username:

Password:

Email:

Pin Code:

Security Question:

Answer:

Account:

Username:

Password:

Email:

Pin Code:

Security Question:

Answer:

A

Account:

Username:

Password:

Email:

Pin Code:

Security Question:

Answer:

Account:

Username:

Password:

Email:

Pin Code:

Security Question:

Answer:

Account:

Username:

Password:

Email:

Pin Code:

Security Question:

Answer:

Account:

Username:

Password:

Email:

Pin Code:

Security Question:

Answer:

Account:

Username:

Password:

Email:

Pin Code:

Security Question:

Answer:

Account:

Username:

Password:

Email:

Pin Code:

Security Question:

Answer:

B

Account:

Username:

Password:

Email:

Pin Code:

Security Question:

Answer:

Account:

Username:

Password:

Email:

Pin Code:

Security Question:

Answer:

Account:

Username:

Password:

Email:

Pin Code:

Security Question:

Answer:

B

Account:

Username:

Password:

Email:

Pin Code:

Security Question:

Answer:

Account:

Username:

Password:

Email:

Pin Code:

Security Question:

Answer:

Account:

Username:

Password:

Email:

Pin Code:

Security Question:

Answer:

B

Account:

Username:

Password:

Email:

Pin Code:

Security Question:

Answer:

Account:

Username:

Password:

Email:

Pin Code:

Security Question:

Answer:

Account:

Username:

Password:

Email:

Pin Code:

Security Question:

Answer:

Account:

Username:

Password:

Email:

Pin Code:

Security Question:

Answer:

Account:

Username:

Password:

Email:

Pin Code:

Security Question:

Answer:

Account:

Username:

Password:

Email:

Pin Code:

Security Question:

Answer:

C |

Account:

Username:

Password:

Email:

Pin Code:

Security Question:

Answer:

Account:

Username:

Password:

Email:

Pin Code:

Security Question:

Answer:

Account:

Username:

Password:

Email:

Pin Code:

Security Question:

Answer:

C

Account: _____

Username: _____

Password: _____

Email: _____

Pin Code: _____

Security Question: _____

Answer: _____

Account: _____

Username: _____

Password: _____

Email: _____

Pin Code: _____

Security Question: _____

Answer: _____

Account: _____

Username: _____

Password: _____

Email: _____

Pin Code: _____

Security Question: _____

Answer: _____

C

Account:

Username:

Password:

Email:

Pin Code:

Security Question:

Answer:

Account:

Username:

Password:

Email:

Pin Code:

Security Question:

Answer:

Account:

Username:

Password:

Email:

Pin Code:

Security Question:

Answer:

C

Account:

Username:

Password:

Email:

Pin Code:

Security Question:

Answer:

Account:

Username:

Password:

Email:

Pin Code:

Security Question:

Answer:

Account:

Username:

Password:

Email:

Pin Code:

Security Question:

Answer:

D

Account:

Username:

Password:

Email:

Pin Code:

Security Question:

Answer:

Account:

Username:

Password:

Email:

Pin Code:

Security Question:

Answer:

Account:

Username:

Password:

Email:

Pin Code:

Security Question:

Answer:

D

Account:

Username:

Password:

Email:

Pin Code:

Security Question:

Answer:

Account:

Username:

Password:

Email:

Pin Code:

Security Question:

Answer:

Account:

Username:

Password:

Email:

Pin Code:

Security Question:

Answer:

D

Account:

Username:

Password:

Email:

Pin Code:

Security Question:

Answer:

Account:

Username:

Password:

Email:

Pin Code:

Security Question:

Answer:

Account:

Username:

Password:

Email:

Pin Code:

Security Question:

Answer:

D

Account:

Username:

Password:

Email:

Pin Code:

Security Question:

Answer:

Account:

Username:

Password:

Email:

Pin Code:

Security Question:

Answer:

Account:

Username:

Password:

Email:

Pin Code:

Security Question:

Answer:

E

Account:

Username:

Password:

Email:

Pin Code:

Security Question:

Answer:

Account:

Username:

Password:

Email:

Pin Code:

Security Question:

Answer:

Account:

Username:

Password:

Email:

Pin Code:

Security Question:

Answer:

E

Account:

Username:

Password:

Email:

Pin Code:

Security Question:

Answer:

Account:

Username:

Password:

Email:

Pin Code:

Security Question:

Answer:

Account:

Username:

Password:

Email:

Pin Code:

Security Question:

Answer:

E

Account:

Username:

Password:

Email:

Pin Code:

Security Question:

Answer:

Account:

Username:

Password:

Email:

Pin Code:

Security Question:

Answer:

Account:

Username:

Password:

Email:

Pin Code:

Security Question:

Answer:

E

Account:

Username:

Password:

Email:

Pin Code:

Security Question:

Answer:

Account:

Username:

Password:

Email:

Pin Code:

Security Question:

Answer:

Account:

Username:

Password:

Email:

Pin Code:

Security Question:

Answer:

F

Account:

Username:

Password:

Email:

Pin Code:

Security Question:

Answer:

Account:

Username:

Password:

Email:

Pin Code:

Security Question:

Answer:

Account:

Username:

Password:

Email:

Pin Code:

Security Question:

Answer:

F

Account:

Username:

Password:

Email:

Pin Code:

Security Question:

Answer:

Account:

Username:

Password:

Email:

Pin Code:

Security Question:

Answer:

Account:

Username:

Password:

Email:

Pin Code:

Security Question:

Answer:

F

Account:

Username:

Password:

Email:

Pin Code:

Security Question:

Answer:

Account:

Username:

Password:

Email:

Pin Code:

Security Question:

Answer:

Account:

Username:

Password:

Email:

Pin Code:

Security Question:

Answer:

F

Account:

Username:

Password:

Email:

Pin Code:

Security Question:

Answer:

Account:

Username:

Password:

Email:

Pin Code:

Security Question:

Answer:

Account:

Username:

Password:

Email:

Pin Code:

Security Question:

Answer:

G

Account:

Username:

Password:

Email:

Pin Code:

Security Question:

Answer:

Account:

Username:

Password:

Email:

Pin Code:

Security Question:

Answer:

Account:

Username:

Password:

Email:

Pin Code:

Security Question:

Answer:

G

Account:

Username:

Password:

Email:

Pin Code:

Security Question:

Answer:

Account:

Username:

Password:

Email:

Pin Code:

Security Question:

Answer:

Account:

Username:

Password:

Email:

Pin Code:

Security Question:

Answer:

G

Account:

Username:

Password:

Email:

Pin Code:

Security Question:

Answer:

Account:

Username:

Password:

Email:

Pin Code:

Security Question:

Answer:

Account:

Username:

Password:

Email:

Pin Code:

Security Question:

Answer:

Account:

Username:

Password:

Email:

Pin Code:

Security Question:

Answer:

Account:

Username:

Password:

Email:

Pin Code:

Security Question:

Answer:

Account:

Username:

Password:

Email:

Pin Code:

Security Question:

Answer:

H |

Account:

Username:

Password:

Email:

Pin Code:

Security Question:

Answer:

Account:

Username:

Password:

Email:

Pin Code:

Security Question:

Answer:

Account:

Username:

Password:

Email:

Pin Code:

Security Question:

Answer:

Account:

Username:

Password:

Email:

Pin Code:

Security Question:

Answer:

Account:

Username:

Password:

Email:

Pin Code:

Security Question:

Answer:

Account:

Username:

Password:

Email:

Pin Code:

Security Question:

Answer:

H

Account:

Username:

Password:

Email:

Pin Code:

Security Question:

Answer:

Account:

Username:

Password:

Email:

Pin Code:

Security Question:

Answer:

Account:

Username:

Password:

Email:

Pin Code:

Security Question:

Answer:

Account:

Username:

Password:

Email:

Pin Code:

Security Question:

Answer:

Account:

Username:

Password:

Email:

Pin Code:

Security Question:

Answer:

Account:

Username:

Password:

Email:

Pin Code:

Security Question:

Answer:

Account:

Username:

Password:

Email:

Pin Code:

Security Question:

Answer:

Account:

Username:

Password:

Email:

Pin Code:

Security Question:

Answer:

Account:

Username:

Password:

Email:

Pin Code:

Security Question:

Answer:

Account: _____

Username: _____

Password: _____

Email: _____

Pin Code: _____

Security Question: _____

Answer: _____

Account: _____

Username: _____

Password: _____

Email: _____

Pin Code: _____

Security Question: _____

Answer: _____

Account: _____

Username: _____

Password: _____

Email: _____

Pin Code: _____

Security Question: _____

Answer: _____

Account:

Username:

Password:

Email:

Pin Code:

Security Question:

Answer:

Account:

Username:

Password:

Email:

Pin Code:

Security Question:

Answer:

Account:

Username:

Password:

Email:

Pin Code:

Security Question:

Answer:

Account: _____

Username: _____

Password: _____

Email: _____

Pin Code: _____

Security Question: _____

Answer: _____

Account: _____

Username: _____

Password: _____

Email: _____

Pin Code: _____

Security Question: _____

Answer: _____

Account: _____

Username: _____

Password: _____

Email: _____

Pin Code: _____

Security Question: _____

Answer: _____

J

Account:

Username:

Password:

Email:

Pin Code:

Security Question:

Answer:

Account:

Username:

Password:

Email:

Pin Code:

Security Question:

Answer:

Account:

Username:

Password:

Email:

Pin Code:

Security Question:

Answer:

Account:

Username:

Password:

Email:

Pin Code:

Security Question:

Answer:

Account:

Username:

Password:

Email:

Pin Code:

Security Question:

Answer:

Account:

Username:

Password:

Email:

Pin Code:

Security Question:

Answer:

J

Account:

Username:

Password:

Email:

Pin Code:

Security Question:

Answer:

Account:

Username:

Password:

Email:

Pin Code:

Security Question:

Answer:

Account:

Username:

Password:

Email:

Pin Code:

Security Question:

Answer:

J

Account:

Username:

Password:

Email:

Pin Code:

Security Question:

Answer:

Account:

Username:

Password:

Email:

Pin Code:

Security Question:

Answer:

Account:

Username:

Password:

Email:

Pin Code:

Security Question:

Answer:

K |

Account:

Username:

Password:

Email:

Pin Code:

Security Question:

Answer:

Account:

Username:

Password:

Email:

Pin Code:

Security Question:

Answer:

Account:

Username:

Password:

Email:

Pin Code:

Security Question:

Answer:

K

Account:

Username:

Password:

Email:

Pin Code:

Security Question:

Answer:

Account:

Username:

Password:

Email:

Pin Code:

Security Question:

Answer:

Account:

Username:

Password:

Email:

Pin Code:

Security Question:

Answer:

K |

Account:

Username:

Password:

Email:

Pin Code:

Security Question:

Answer:

Account:

Username:

Password:

Email:

Pin Code:

Security Question:

Answer:

Account:

Username:

Password:

Email:

Pin Code:

Security Question:

Answer:

K

Account:

Username:

Password:

Email:

Pin Code:

Security Question:

Answer:

Account:

Username:

Password:

Email:

Pin Code:

Security Question:

Answer:

Account:

Username:

Password:

Email:

Pin Code:

Security Question:

Answer:

L

Account:

Username:

Password:

Email:

Pin Code:

Security Question:

Answer:

Account:

Username:

Password:

Email:

Pin Code:

Security Question:

Answer:

Account:

Username:

Password:

Email:

Pin Code:

Security Question:

Answer:

L

_____

Account: _____

Username: _____

Password: _____

Email: _____

Pin Code: _____

Security Question: _____

Answer: _____

Account: _____

Username: _____

Password: _____

Email: _____

Pin Code: _____

Security Question: _____

Answer: _____

Account: _____

Username: _____

Password: _____

Email: _____

Pin Code: _____

Security Question: _____

Answer: _____

L

Account:

Username:

Password:

Email:

Pin Code:

Security Question:

Answer:

Account:

Username:

Password:

Email:

Pin Code:

Security Question:

Answer:

Account:

Username:

Password:

Email:

Pin Code:

Security Question:

Answer:

L

Account:

Username:

Password:

Email:

Pin Code:

Security Question:

Answer:

Account:

Username:

Password:

Email:

Pin Code:

Security Question:

Answer:

Account:

Username:

Password:

Email:

Pin Code:

Security Question:

Answer:

M

Account:

Username:

Password:

Email:

Pin Code:

Security Question:

Answer:

Account:

Username:

Password:

Email:

Pin Code:

Security Question:

Answer:

Account:

Username:

Password:

Email:

Pin Code:

Security Question:

Answer:

M

Account:

Username:

Password:

Email:

Pin Code:

Security Question:

Answer:

Account:

Username:

Password:

Email:

Pin Code:

Security Question:

Answer:

Account:

Username:

Password:

Email:

Pin Code:

Security Question:

Answer:

M

Account:

Username:

Password:

Email:

Pin Code:

Security Question:

Answer:

Account:

Username:

Password:

Email:

Pin Code:

Security Question:

Answer:

Account:

Username:

Password:

Email:

Pin Code:

Security Question:

Answer:

M

Account: _____

Username: _____

Password: _____

Email: _____

Pin Code: _____

Security Question: _____

Answer: _____

Account: _____

Username: _____

Password: _____

Email: _____

Pin Code: _____

Security Question: _____

Answer: _____

Account: _____

Username: _____

Password: _____

Email: _____

Pin Code: _____

Security Question: _____

Answer: _____

N

Account:

Username:

Password:

Email:

Pin Code:

Security Question:

Answer:

Account:

Username:

Password:

Email:

Pin Code:

Security Question:

Answer:

Account:

Username:

Password:

Email:

Pin Code:

Security Question:

Answer:

Account:

Username:

Password:

Email:

Pin Code:

Security Question:

Answer:

Account:

Username:

Password:

Email:

Pin Code:

Security Question:

Answer:

Account:

Username:

Password:

Email:

Pin Code:

Security Question:

Answer:

N

Account:

Username:

Password:

Email:

Pin Code:

Security Question:

Answer:

Account:

Username:

Password:

Email:

Pin Code:

Security Question:

Answer:

Account:

Username:

Password:

Email:

Pin Code:

Security Question:

Answer:

Account:

Username:

Password:

Email:

Pin Code:

Security Question:

Answer:

Account:

Username:

Password:

Email:

Pin Code:

Security Question:

Answer:

Account:

Username:

Password:

Email:

Pin Code:

Security Question:

Answer:

O |

Account:

Username:

Password:

Email:

Pin Code:

Security Question:

Answer:

Account:

Username:

Password:

Email:

Pin Code:

Security Question:

Answer:

Account:

Username:

Password:

Email:

Pin Code:

Security Question:

Answer:

_____ | 0

Account: _____

Username: _____

Password: _____

Email: _____

Pin Code: _____

Security Question: _____

Answer: _____

_____

Account: _____

Username: _____

Password: _____

Email: _____

Pin Code: _____

Security Question: _____

Answer: _____

_____

Account: _____

Username: _____

Password: _____

Email: _____

Pin Code: _____

Security Question: _____

Answer: _____

_____

0 |＿＿＿＿＿＿＿＿＿＿＿＿＿

Account:

Username:

Password:

Email:

Pin Code:

Security Question:

Answer:

Account:

Username:

Password:

Email:

Pin Code:

Security Question:

Answer:

Account:

Username:

Password:

Email:

Pin Code:

Security Question:

Answer:

Account:

Username:

Password:

Email:

Pin Code:

Security Question:

Answer:

Account:

Username:

Password:

Email:

Pin Code:

Security Question:

Answer:

Account:

Username:

Password:

Email:

Pin Code:

Security Question:

Answer:

P

Account:

Username:

Password:

Email:

Pin Code:

Security Question:

Answer:

Account:

Username:

Password:

Email:

Pin Code:

Security Question:

Answer:

Account:

Username:

Password:

Email:

Pin Code:

Security Question:

Answer:

P

Account:

Username:

Password:

Email:

Pin Code:

Security Question:

Answer:

Account:

Username:

Password:

Email:

Pin Code:

Security Question:

Answer:

Account:

Username:

Password:

Email:

Pin Code:

Security Question:

Answer:

P

Account:

Username:

Password:

Email:

Pin Code:

Security Question:

Answer:

Account:

Username:

Password:

Email:

Pin Code:

Security Question:

Answer:

Account:

Username:

Password:

Email:

Pin Code:

Security Question:

Answer:

Account:

Username:

Password:

Email:

Pin Code:

Security Question:

Answer:

Account:

Username:

Password:

Email:

Pin Code:

Security Question:

Answer:

Account:

Username:

Password:

Email:

Pin Code:

Security Question:

Answer:

Q

Account:

Username:

Password:

Email:

Pin Code:

Security Question:

Answer:

Account:

Username:

Password:

Email:

Pin Code:

Security Question:

Answer:

Account:

Username:

Password:

Email:

Pin Code:

Security Question:

Answer:

Q

Account:

Username:

Password:

Email:

Pin Code:

Security Question:

Answer:

Account:

Username:

Password:

Email:

Pin Code:

Security Question:

Answer:

Account:

Username:

Password:

Email:

Pin Code:

Security Question:

Answer:

Q

Account:

Username:

Password:

Email:

Pin Code:

Security Question:

Answer:

Account:

Username:

Password:

Email:

Pin Code:

Security Question:

Answer:

Account:

Username:

Password:

Email:

Pin Code:

Security Question:

Answer:

Q

Account:

Username:

Password:

Email:

Pin Code:

Security Question:

Answer:

Account:

Username:

Password:

Email:

Pin Code:

Security Question:

Answer:

Account:

Username:

Password:

Email:

Pin Code:

Security Question:

Answer:

R

Account:

Username:

Password:

Email:

Pin Code:

Security Question:

Answer:

Account:

Username:

Password:

Email:

Pin Code:

Security Question:

Answer:

Account:

Username:

Password:

Email:

Pin Code:

Security Question:

Answer:

R

Account:

Username:

Password:

Email:

Pin Code:

Security Question:

Answer:

Account:

Username:

Password:

Email:

Pin Code:

Security Question:

Answer:

Account:

Username:

Password:

Email:

Pin Code:

Security Question:

Answer:

R

Account:

Username:

Password:

Email:

Pin Code:

Security Question:

Answer:

Account:

Username:

Password:

Email:

Pin Code:

Security Question:

Answer:

Account:

Username:

Password:

Email:

Pin Code:

Security Question:

Answer:

R

Account:

Username:

Password:

Email:

Pin Code:

Security Question:

Answer:

Account:

Username:

Password:

Email:

Pin Code:

Security Question:

Answer:

Account:

Username:

Password:

Email:

Pin Code:

Security Question:

Answer:

S

Account:

Username:

Password:

Email:

Pin Code:

Security Question:

Answer:

Account:

Username:

Password:

Email:

Pin Code:

Security Question:

Answer:

Account:

Username:

Password:

Email:

Pin Code:

Security Question:

Answer:

S

Account:

Username:

Password:

Email:

Pin Code:

Security Question:

Answer:

Account:

Username:

Password:

Email:

Pin Code:

Security Question:

Answer:

Account:

Username:

Password:

Email:

Pin Code:

Security Question:

Answer:

S

Account:

Username:

Password:

Email:

Pin Code:

Security Question:

Answer:

Account:

Username:

Password:

Email:

Pin Code:

Security Question:

Answer:

Account:

Username:

Password:

Email:

Pin Code:

Security Question:

Answer:

S

Account: _____

Username: _____

Password: _____

Email: _____

Pin Code: _____

Security Question: _____

Answer: _____

Account: _____

Username: _____

Password: _____

Email: _____

Pin Code: _____

Security Question: _____

Answer: _____

Account: _____

Username: _____

Password: _____

Email: _____

Pin Code: _____

Security Question: _____

Answer: _____

T |

Account:

Username:

Password:

Email:

Pin Code:

Security Question:

Answer:

Account:

Username:

Password:

Email:

Pin Code:

Security Question:

Answer:

Account:

Username:

Password:

Email:

Pin Code:

Security Question:

Answer:

T

Account:

Username:

Password:

Email:

Pin Code:

Security Question:

Answer:

Account:

Username:

Password:

Email:

Pin Code:

Security Question:

Answer:

Account:

Username:

Password:

Email:

Pin Code:

Security Question:

Answer:

T |

Account:

Username:

Password:

Email:

Pin Code:

Security Question:

Answer:

Account:

Username:

Password:

Email:

Pin Code:

Security Question:

Answer:

Account:

Username:

Password:

Email:

Pin Code:

Security Question:

Answer:

T

Account:

Username:

Password:

Email:

Pin Code:

Security Question:

Answer:

Account:

Username:

Password:

Email:

Pin Code:

Security Question:

Answer:

Account:

Username:

Password:

Email:

Pin Code:

Security Question:

Answer:

U

Account:

Username:

Password:

Email:

Pin Code:

Security Question:

Answer:

Account:

Username:

Password:

Email:

Pin Code:

Security Question:

Answer:

Account:

Username:

Password:

Email:

Pin Code:

Security Question:

Answer:

U

Account:

Username:

Password:

Email:

Pin Code:

Security Question:

Answer:

Account:

Username:

Password:

Email:

Pin Code:

Security Question:

Answer:

Account:

Username:

Password:

Email:

Pin Code:

Security Question:

Answer:

U

Account:

Username:

Password:

Email:

Pin Code:

Security Question:

Answer:

Account:

Username:

Password:

Email:

Pin Code:

Security Question:

Answer:

Account:

Username:

Password:

Email:

Pin Code:

Security Question:

Answer:

Account: _____

Username: _____

Password: _____

Email: _____

Pin Code: _____

Security Question: _____

Answer: _____

Account: _____

Username: _____

Password: _____

Email: _____

Pin Code: _____

Security Question: _____

Answer: _____

Account: _____

Username: _____

Password: _____

Email: _____

Pin Code: _____

Security Question: _____

Answer: _____

V

Account:

Username:

Password:

Email:

Pin Code:

Security Question:

Answer:

Account:

Username:

Password:

Email:

Pin Code:

Security Question:

Answer:

Account:

Username:

Password:

Email:

Pin Code:

Security Question:

Answer:

V

Account:

Username:

Password:

Email:

Pin Code:

Security Question:

Answer:

Account:

Username:

Password:

Email:

Pin Code:

Security Question:

Answer:

Account:

Username:

Password:

Email:

Pin Code:

Security Question:

Answer:

V

Account:

Username:

Password:

Email:

Pin Code:

Security Question:

Answer:

Account:

Username:

Password:

Email:

Pin Code:

Security Question:

Answer:

Account:

Username:

Password:

Email:

Pin Code:

Security Question:

Answer:

V

Account:

Username:

Password:

Email:

Pin Code:

Security Question:

Answer:

Account:

Username:

Password:

Email:

Pin Code:

Security Question:

Answer:

Account:

Username:

Password:

Email:

Pin Code:

Security Question:

Answer:

W |

Account:

Username:

Password:

Email:

Pin Code:

Security Question:

Answer:

Account:

Username:

Password:

Email:

Pin Code:

Security Question:

Answer:

Account:

Username:

Password:

Email:

Pin Code:

Security Question:

Answer:

W

Account: _____

Username: _____

Password: _____

Email: _____

Pin Code: _____

Security Question: _____

Answer: _____

Account: _____

Username: _____

Password: _____

Email: _____

Pin Code: _____

Security Question: _____

Answer: _____

Account: _____

Username: _____

Password: _____

Email: _____

Pin Code: _____

Security Question: _____

Answer: _____

W |
_____

Account:

Username:

Password:

Email:

Pin Code:

Security Question:

Answer:

Account:

Username:

Password:

Email:

Pin Code:

Security Question:

Answer:

Account:

Username:

Password:

Email:

Pin Code:

Security Question:

Answer:

W

Account:

Username:

Password:

Email:

Pin Code:

Security Question:

Answer:

Account:

Username:

Password:

Email:

Pin Code:

Security Question:

Answer:

Account:

Username:

Password:

Email:

Pin Code:

Security Question:

Answer:

XYZ

Account:

Username:

Password:

Email:

Pin Code:

Security Question:

Answer:

Account:

Username:

Password:

Email:

Pin Code:

Security Question:

Answer:

Account:

Username:

Password:

Email:

Pin Code:

Security Question:

Answer:

XYZ

_____

Account: _____

Username: _____

Password: _____

Email: _____

Pin Code: _____

Security Question: _____

Answer: _____

Account: _____

Username: _____

Password: _____

Email: _____

Pin Code: _____

Security Question: _____

Answer: _____

Account: _____

Username: _____

Password: _____

Email: _____

Pin Code: _____

Security Question: _____

Answer: _____

XYZ

Account:

Username:

Password:

Email:

Pin Code:

Security Question:

Answer:

Account:

Username:

Password:

Email:

Pin Code:

Security Question:

Answer:

Account:

Username:

Password:

Email:

Pin Code:

Security Question:

Answer:

XYZ

_____

Account: _____

Username: _____

Password: _____

Email: _____

Pin Code: _____

Security Question: _____

Answer: _____

Account: _____

Username: _____

Password: _____

Email: _____

Pin Code: _____

Security Question: _____

Answer: _____

Account: _____

Username: _____

Password: _____

Email: _____

Pin Code: _____

Security Question: _____

Answer: _____

Made in the USA
Monee, IL
07 November 2022

17287624R00057